MW00641751

FROM MEMPHIS & PEKING

For Nina
with best wishes
Barbara Chase-Riboud
Paris 76

FROM MEMPHIS & PEKING

POEMS BY

B. CHASE-RIBOUD

RANDOM HOUSE
NEW YORK

 Published in the United
States by Random House, Inc.,
New York, and simultaneously in Canada
by Random House of Canada Limited,
Toronto.

Library of Congress Cataloging in Publication Data
Chase-Riboud, Barbara.
From Memphis and Peking; poems.
I. Title.
PS3553.H336F7 811'.5'4 73-20085
ISBN 0-394-48899-7

Manufactured in the United States
of America

9 8 7 5 4 3 2

First Edition

FOR ANNA, AGNES
AND VIVIAN

CONTENTS

MEMPHIS

ANNA

LETTERS

MEMPHIS

WHY DID WE LEAVE ZANZIBAR?

Dark haloed sister
Penumbric jewel
Burning in dry tobacco leaf beauty
Brittle and flaking discontent
Eyes damned with the silt of disappointment
Lodged and sheltered in Public Housing
Celled there tapping in Morse code on the bars of the mind:
The unspeakable that resounds through
The landscape of your nerve ends like orgasm
Long-fingered, long-necked
Delicate wristed and ankled sister
Wide-hipped and smelling of honey
Eyes echoing hollow words and unremembered places
Fingers stuttering, tearing
And wrapping themselves around
The essential question:

Why did we leave Zanzibar?

Something in the line of the back spells
The irredeemable exhaustion of trying to make ends meet
Those two butt ends of our amputated history
Cauterized on the hot iron of self-hate
Lusting after self-destruction
That we find in split vaginas
Smeared with the muck of barbarians
Birthing a race of orphans and madmen
When we could have stayed on the beach
Heads severed and wombs filled with sand
Clutching our ancestors
Rejoicing in sterility
Reveling in abortion
Resplendent with infanticide
Cursing the living with the last breath of strangled children
You say we had no choice:

There is always one alternative
to rape and every woman knows it

Dark-breathed sister
Sinister survival worshiper
Ready with the sword to smite the suicides
Jailer for our prison-makers
Grinding down our men with religion-pocked
Grins of satisfaction (Jesus Saves)
Crushing our defenseless sons with the jawbone of that
  Jew's cross
(Dazed and concussed, they stumble into the street to play
  stickball
Driving their fathers mad with grief and shame
So that their rage is spent in our bodies
(Or better still, the wives and daughters of the enemy)
And how we both glory in it
Smack our lips in rutting satisfaction
Tasting curdled blood and milk
Left standing in the sun too long
By absent-minded missionaries

Benedictus qui venit in
nomine Domini

Sassy, sweet-voiced sister
Moon-browed and night-mouthed
In deepest song
Lying on your back in cathedrals
Content that another night has passed
Without murder
Lying on your back in cathedrals
Masturbating with the true cross (Sweet Jesus)
While black men thrash around with white flesh
Listening for your hysterical screams resounding in the
  tabernacle
Staining stained glass: those technicolor prisms of some
  Middle Eastern legend
And over all, Cleopatra's asp hovers:
Sliding between legs
That perpetually open route to power:
Posing the essential question on split tongue:

Why did we leave Zanzibar?
Sweet fragrant mango-stenched beach
Breasts pressed flat against steamed sand
Seeping through sieve-like flesh
Carrying carats of ancestor dust
Rattling like pearls in oyster shells

Sleek, earth-dyed sister
Madness glistening at your throat
We could have stayed on the beach
Clinging to the rocks like bats
REFUSING TO MOVE OUR WOMBS
Scraping them with flint
Soaking the continent with the holy blood of martyrs
Plum-lipped sister
Sad and wild-eyed with my reflection
I touch one apricot breast
As you touch one brassy one
And we gaze into each other's eyes
Like the criminals that we are
Dark brown gall rising to the surface like oil on water
Casting up that bottle-wrapped question
Flung into the sea by some desperate hand so many
murders ago.

Why did we leave Zanzibar?

COME WITH ME

Come
With
Me.
Into my deep dry bower
Filled with saffron, musk and Gulheina
And I will
Raise you up and lead you on

I will sing you
A Song
In a clear low voice
A voice of Africa and
India
A voice of the Arapaho Indians
A voice of
Scotland and Wales

Come
With
Me.
Into my garden
Draped with Spanish moss, honeysuckle and wisteria
And I will
Raise you up and lead you on
And I will tell you
A Tale
In a whisper
A tale of Africa and
India
A tale of the Arapaho Indians
A tale of
Scotland and Wales

Come
With
Me.
Into my reflecting pool
Filled with iris, silvered fish and sapphire pebbles
And I will
Raise you up and lead you on
I will dance you
A Dance
Quietly
A dance of Africa and
India
A dance of the Arapaho Indians

A dance of
Scotland and Wales

Come
With
Me.
Into my orchard
Filled with peach, cherry and blue raisins
And I will
Raise you up and lead you on
I will play you
The Calf Skin
Softly
The gourd of Africa and the
Sitar of India
The flute of the Arapaho Indians
And the bagpipes of
Scotland and Wales

Come
Tremble in my arms
You will be a bay leaf shaken
And I will
Raise you up and lead you on
I will take you in and let you out
I will leave you come and make you go
I will let you down and bring you up
I will follow you and then go back
I will quit you and then catch up
You will arrive and you will depart
You will begin and you will end
You will fall down and
I will pick you up and turn you
Round
And
Lead
You
Home.

IF I LONG FOR THAT OASIS

If I long
For that oasis I call home
That white disk edged in
Cold bursting neon
Remember this:
My last refuge is you, my love
Primed for the onrush of my curious
And dense body
That invades your privacy
Like the echo of the pulses of
Bird wings
One second after flight
When the air is still troubled
And its space hasn't been displaced
By excited titters of dry gas
While the ghost of expelled breath
Still hovers in the heated zephyr
A prediction of turbulence to come
If only every four hundred years
Like the Phoenix
I rise to greet you
So stubborn, needful, greedy, determined
To devour you with dark
While you blind me with light
You'll remember this battle . . .
Through the dry ice of concentric hells
As hoary as snowbound Leningrad
You'll remember this battle . . .
How exhausted, my love
Will we be
In the end?

ALL REVERENCE TO HER

I

When the last cock crows and the last bell chimes and
The morning star excommunicates night and the moon
Pales and the last nightmare fades and the sun
Rises intact watching as we spit morning
Blood: Mouthwash of the Western World
I'll turn my head on my pillow and
Salute *that power that exists*
In all of us in the form
Of Illusion Reverence
All Reverence to
Her Reverence
Reverence to
Her all
Rever-
ence
to
H
e
r
.

II

When the last politician has murdered the last son and
The last child has starved for the last grains of
Rice and the last absolution has bloodied the
Last Holy Land and the last prayer leaves
The last bullet-punctured heart neatly
I'll turn my head on my pillow and
Salute *that power that exists*
In all of us in the form
Of Illusion Reverence
All Reverence to
Her Reverence
Reverence to
Her all
Rever-
ence
to
H
e
r
.

III

When the last child has sucked the last breast of the
Last corpse and orphans curse the government with
Their mother's name in this last nation on the
Last planet skewing in hara-kiri as man's
Last foot touches the last moon
I'll turn my head on my pillow and
Salute *that power that exists*
In all of us in the form
Of Illusion Reverence
All Reverence to
Her Reverence
Reverence to
Her all
Rever-
ence
to
H
e
r
.

IV

When the last kiss sates one last rapturous paroxysm
The Race spinning and burning in fear as much as
Lust: Life's last illustrations receding into
Time and space inventing pretensions with
The last mouthing of love's last word
I'll turn my head towards you and
Salute *that power that exists*
In all of us in the form
Of Illusion Reverence
All Reverence to
Her Reverence
Reverence to
Her all
Rever-
ence
to
H
e
r
.

BATHERS

Bathers
In a new and unpolluted sea
Fresh from vision
You and I
You and I
New
New
Emerging
Clinking like metal
Shiny on the sand
As wave-washed copper pennies
Anchored by beach lizards
Weighted in shrouds of
Smooth rose pebbles
Attached to
Slow-rolling flying kites
Separated by a
Gritty breeze
That winds down
The space
Between us
As irrefutable as
The Great Chinese Wall . . .
Evaporating sea tears
On you
Sea tears that dry
Leaving small white
Circles of brine
Not like my tears
That remain
Forever
Undried
As I walk back into that
New and unpolluted sea
Fresh from vision

You and I
You and I
Old
Old
Converging
In the ooze of
Radiolarian skeletons
On the bottom
Of the Arabian Sea.

THE SEAL

Stranger when you place your delicate hands on me write your dreams on my left side undo my hair suddenly and for no good reason stranger when you place your mouth hot as Alexandrian sand that cools my parched throat like well-water place your mouth on my mouths one and then the other until I taste myself stranger when you weight my flesh desperately burden it politely mold it and knead it and penetrate it asking and giving no quarter stranger when you take from me that sound primordial which is silence quits me with the stealth of a rain-forest beast fleeing stranger when with a finger I trace your lips that debauched mouth (voluptuary) (you) (egoist) with that cynical left side and that right side dissolved in sensibility stranger when I tongue your breast as hard and as flat as outlaw country trail your rivers and streams your banks and valleys to my final destination stranger when your nostrils narrow your cries escape cries I extract with feral tenderness you! your arrogant silences silenced stranger when I scan your face beauty-ravaged-male-body the Rector rectified done in under mine/ reversed when that hour strikes I think ah well well-loved stranger when will we be friends?

PEARLS

I spit them out:
These pearls
And falling they turned to blood
Tubercular stain collecting
In a bouquet under my chin
And night passed and day
Regret passed and desire
Life passed and love
And dying alone
Holding my own hand
I opened my mouth to receive the Holy Ghost
And the last pearl fell
I took it on my tongue and found
A ruby as sweet as wine.

LE LIT

Sullen blizzard of white linen
Lying rumpled
Under the morning sun
Last night's pressed flesh
Still glowing like the flickering shadows
Of a silent movie
Contours still raging like burnt-out onion skin
Dry and flaking with
Tiny ridges where a thousand drummed dreams
Swam like microbes

Pale riderless white
Turning as the sun turns
Into a melancholy monument

Spent sheets with the pillows on the floor
Whistling like Memnon at dawn
Blue-veined as Carrara marble
Frozen into pompous History
A tombstone fashioned by some
Second-rate sculptor
To support his family of ten

Summits like a crumpled Sphinx
Take on a life of their own
Mesas and mountains rise and fall
Lake bottoms and craters breathe and sigh
Strangled and tortured in the
Tangled limbs of a forlorn and
More than slightly ridiculous lagoon
A neglected memorial from the Great War
Expensively made only to be disfigured by
Disrespectful children

I ache to soothe those troubled peaks of lust
To calm the kind contusions of the night
At least to lay a wreath on you
And sit silently
In my cripple's chair
Relieved to be alive but not happy
Straining to read
The half-effaced and fading legend
In Roman letters . . .

HERE LIED.

LOVE CAN DIE

Love can die.
I never knew that
I never knew that
Until
Now

Sitting across the table from you

My heart
A hard green apple
Swaying in the breeze
Of petitions and denunciations
Without falling
My heart
A steel ball-bearing
Gliding smoothly round
The clogs and pistons of
Disillusionment.

Love can die.
I never knew that
I never knew that
Until
Now

Sitting across the table from you

My eyes
Two raisins
Dried beyond relief
Beyond any juice
That lovely wine-love dark and pungent
That still might spill
Slipping down my throat like
Fingers sneaking around my breast
A leaping heart
Stunned into silence

Love can die.
I never knew that

I never knew that
Until
Now

Sitting across the table from you

My lips
That once took yours on mine like breath
Stacked like a deck of cards
The fool strangled
My clenched teeth black coals
My tongue a steel oven raging
To tell you to Stop
To Stop
To Stop
Before I have to tell you myself that

Love can die.
I never knew that
I never knew that
I never knew that
I never knew that
I never knew that
I never knew that
I never knew that
I never knew that

THE ALBINO

The absence of color
Is that the answer
To a moral question?
White African
Walking negative
Are you
Magic?

An ancestor called back
To prove the soul lives?
White African
Walking negative
Are you
Holy?
The sacred circle of the
Tantra?
White African
Walking negative
Are you
Proof?
Of the exception
Which proves the rule
Like the Hermaphrodite?
If color exists then
The absence of color must exist
As well
As a single face becomes dual
In a mirror
As a single body becomes dual
In a shadow
As a single thought becomes
Past and present
In the mind's eye
As the only difference between
The seen and the unseen is
Love
I am as male as I am female
I am as white as I am black
There is no difference
Between She and He
Between You and Me
You are as female as you are male
You are as black as you are white
Together we are
One

Yet together
We are not
One
But as love knows
Only love knows
Our subtle differences
Let there be
No doubt
About this
The absence of color
Is that the answer
To a moral question?

I'VE TRAVELED

I've traveled.
Across the dewy small of your back
Down the ridge of backbone like a lonely skier
Smoothed steely flanks trembling
Held on to your sighs
Kissed damp hair blinding me
Frail childlike hair, now darkened
But you were so blond
When we were young.

We've traveled.
Left many a mauve flower
Wizened on blue sheets
Left many a moan
Echoing down dark hallways:
Night sounds that crept past
The nursery where we slept

The clutched and rapturous
Dreams of children.

Together we've traveled.
Fingers clasped in that death grip
Of sibling love
Beyond the Pale
Beyond the pale
Poppy you press again and again
Into the perfume of a wearied heart
That gleams and creacks
This dusty afternoon.

Beside me, you've traveled.
Followed me down steep slippery stairways
Into the entrails of that reprobate mansion
Demolished abandoned and condemned by all
Thus the most perfect and intact of all places
Where at last arrived in the barred light of your cell
I brush the cobwebs from your eyes and lips
Press my hand on secret parts
Rest my head on an innocent breast shuddering:

Brother,
I've loved you.

ON HEARING OF A DEATH IN PRISON

For George Jackson Blois, August 21st 1971

I heard
A wailing mournful sacred
Song
A bitter screaming humping

Song
A positively displeased Nigger's
Song
A Maximum Security
Song
A river of bile
Har-
Monica fresh filled with
Salty blood
I taste it
Myself
Now.

I heard
A silent Georgia
Bad lands
Song
Flat-out
In the damned black
Of the American sky
White speckled with
Filthy stars
Spangled
Cold as ice
Cold as Hell
Frozen over
Out there
One
Dies

I heard
A teeth-grinding heart stripping lover's
Song
A fine jazz ricochet of desire
Drizzling gall
Sex-starved and slave-chained in
Songs of sixpence

The inherited penalty of pain
Passed from father to son in
Songs
Of penitentiaries:
San Rafael
Folsom
San Quentin
Alcatraz
Soledad.

I heard
A never-ending song of
Solitude
Eleven years of putrid cement tomb
Nailed down
With bullets
And the
Constitution
For sixty-seven dollars net
A song eleven years to sing in
Solitary confinement
Excrement thrown
The total death of pride
The soul-destroying body search
A rape of every aperture
A curse so foul
Men cry

I heard
Black notes on lined paper
Barred
Dropping wounded days
Of manhood lost
In gut-punctured-spine-shattered
Death
Death of the spirit
Death of the bowels

Death in the white heat
Of a charred sunlit court
So lonely it seizes
The heart
That hoarded dreamed-of
Moment of Life
The last.

I heard
A clamorous clapper-tongued
Sound
The holocaust of Easter Week
A trenchant trill
Quivering in heat over
The Entire Race
Blue desert women
Wind and sand whipped pillars
Stretching across Africa
Tattooed hands held over
That obscene opening
Kohl-ed eyes weeping
Black tears for Black Men
Red veils aspired in Rage
In Rage, In Rage, In Rage

I heard
A Song
So rich in gut and blood
That any sperm would flower there
And any Song
Rejoice in being
Not
For singing.

GOING TO MEMPHIS

I

I'm leaving this place
Quitting this watery catalogue
Held sweetly on this river by my boat
Lacquered in black and white and covered with
Designs of swords and cups, wands and pentacles
My hair trails in the reflected sky while
My men's oars drag in the pearly wrack
I weigh a pomegranate on the scale before me
A bushel of sunflower seeds to the left of me
A basket of shellfish to the right of me
A fountain flows in back of me and a palm crowns me
Nevertheless we do not eat nor drink nor stop for rest
We are going to Memphis
I gaze into the saffron mirror of Venus
The cups to the left of me and the cubes to the right
The twelve fruited tree shades me and a white pillar crosses me
The day passes and quivering heat visions
Mingle with the steam of my breath as
I keen to the rhythm of the rowers while
The sun blows on my eyelids
Where love comes up poppy-red (what joy cultivated) and
My eyes become as unseeing as baked amber
Set in the deadly cross of a gilded past as
We pass forgotten places and they wave to me from the
Shore
We pass remembered places and they wave to me from the
shore
We pass dreadful places and they wave to me from the shore
We pass nameless places and they wave to me from the shore
My cry carried by herons unfurls across water:
I'm going to Memphis, I won't be back this way
I'm going to Memphis, I won't be back this way
I'm going to Memphis, I won't be back this way
I'm going to Memphis.

II

I'm leaving this place
Cheeks swollen with puffed breaths of desperate life
Swaddled in silk sails embroidered delicately by infant hands
I glide from mistake to mistake
Raising my colors insolently for everyone to see
For I am the Signifier
The way is in me.
My convicts need no compass and my sails no wind
For this river runs deep and this river runs straight
This river runs wide and this river runs true
No steel and concrete dam can alter its course
No explosions of man-made trivia arrest its current
I hum to myself softly and pluck on a ram's head
My eyes keep to his and not to the shore for I need no sign
The moon rises behind me
The path opens in front of me
The mountains stay to the left of me
The stream remains to the right of me
IHVH crowns me and Ankh crosses me with a kiss
Eclipse comes and the orb of the world dissolves in a pentagram
Comets kiss stars and neighboring universes fiance hotly
Watching ellipsoids spin and meteorites wed asteroids
Colliding like a panicked crowd at the fire exit of space as
We pass old friends and they wave to me from the shore
We pass worn loves and they wave to me from the shore
We pass my children and they wave to me from the shore
We pass my lover and he waves to me from the shore
My cry carried by sparrow hawks unfurls across waters:
I'm going to Memphis, I won't be back this way
I'm going to Memphis, I won't be back this way
I'm going to Memphis, I won't be back this way
I'm going to Memphis.

III

I'm leaving this place
Nostrils exhaling rare incense

Intoxicating sea gulls into suicide dives against my chest
As I watch luminous crabs make love in the deep
A felluca, sodden sails big-bellied with sin, hung low from
God knows what heathen voyage makes a figure eight in salute
I sigh and light my pipe in the modern dawn
And play cards with the Hierophant
His triple crown reversed, his scepter triply crossed
And I win which makes him triply cross
And Anibus sees it from his tower and laughs in his harelip
Inviting dawn while I drink the wreath before me and crush the
wheel
Devour the lion to my right and strangle the wolf to my left
Pick the red rose that crowns me and bloodied become very
silly
Giggling and snickering behind my hand, panting and screaming
Like a wailing wind-played Aeolian harp unstrung
Battling in my simple-minded way hysteria and cataplexy
Insanity, scotoma and the Devil
Mortifying my own flesh and munching icy emeralds
I fish from the side of the boat with my hair
(They melt in my mouth like rock candy)
Exhausted, I turn and meekly sleep the dreamless sleep of
beasts and children
The wings of the Phoenix press against my bankrupt mouth
his head on one breast as
We pass the shore of the dead and it heaves sand at us
We pass the end of the world and it vomits burning pyres
We pass the other side of truth and don't recognize it
We pass the wretched of the earth devouring the dogs of the
rich
My cry haunts me in the mute eyes of black eagles
I'm going to Memphis, I won't be back this way
I'm going to Memphis, I won't be back this way
I'm going to Memphis, I won't be back this way
I'm going to Memphis.

IV

I've left this place
Become as liquid and as salty as the water that carries me
Descending the depths like a sea-diver umbilically attached
To a past I never loved, I see the beginning of the end
And enter into it with joy
Plunge into a tunnel, so wide, so long, so deep that
All conversation stops and everyone becomes very serious
Sucking the rancid breath of life until
Leaving this black, our pupils focusing not on any light
A silver temple rises up like lightning whistling in the dark
Holy metal veiled in lily-roots snorting downwards
Making caverns for petulant ghosts
Reflections etched in black and white on its sinuous surface
Sculpted like lava cooled by the brine of sea winds
Smooth as a phallus worn by a million hands
Warm and heavy metal more luxurious than lust
Raised on a courtyard laid in Byzantine love-amulets
A boulevard of unleavened and unrepentant and unbaptized
 souls
Oscillating in the nacreous light that is neither sun nor moon
Standing in a Time which is neither day nor night
In a climate which is neither summer nor winter
In a sky only burnt-out stars could invent: the negative of light
On a plain as level and as flat as fate.
My criminals lift their oars in salute oozing molten semen from
 the dead sea
(Sweat from the sons of father-less ghosts)
The keys slide like maggots down the hollow hanging sleeve of
 the Angel
The Yod crosses me illuminating my left side
Blinding the Sphinx on my right side and hallowing Zero
Crowning me in blinking, glowing ectoplasmic neon forever as
I rise to greet this musical cathedral arching as if to greet a lover
Nipples hard and heart bursting whispering:
Memphis I'm arrived.

For I am the Signifier
The way is in me
And now is the time.

[Dedicated to Victoria Reiter
with thanks for her unswerving support
and encouragement for this book.
B.C.R. Paris, November 1, 1973]

ANNA

ANNA

1.

I remember
You
Anna
I walk this narrow brick alley
Named after you and
Look for myself
I come with someone you'd like
A friend
A lover
I try to see through this
White clapboard house
Into my beginnings
Any history will do
For those who have none
It seems you lived so long here
They named the street after you
McWard Street
House number seven
Kingston, Toronto
Ontario
Canada
The end of the line
Great-grandmother
Did you know?

2.

I remember
You
Anna
1945
You must have been
Eighty-five or even older
It hardly matters
And I?
I was six
Could I have known the word for
Empress?
Imperious old lady
Amber-colored
Chinese perfume bottle
Engraved with jewels
(Beautiful jewels, I thought)
Set off by black crepe
Hair straight as a song
Disciplined
Into a silk cap
You looked at me and murmured
"Too dark.
She'll never be beautiful."
Oh Great-grandmother
The blood
You let
With that
Offhand remark
The absolute wound
That saw
My life flow
Out
Sweet dreams of myself
Shot free like stars spinning
From another galaxy
Great-grandmother
Did you know?

3.

I remember
You
Anna
Queen
How could you have begun
In slavery?
Staring with unfocused infant eyes
As your mother dipped her hand into
Blood and drank
And fled
Swaddled like a tiny Egyptian on her back
Clinging to her frightened heart
Did you feel the stars rush by?
Feel your mother's straining lungs
Exhaling frosted panic onto the night?
How does one run to
Fate?
Why do some not
Bend?
What made your mother
Bloody herself?
An overseer's rape?
A husband sold?
A child born not free?
The ache of the African sun in her eyes?
The white sand of Nairobi
Shifting under her feet?
Did she remember
The Nile?
Was it a hot breeze off
The Sahara?
Could it have been a sigh from
The Indian Ocean?
Great-grandmother
Did you know?

4.

I remember
You
Anna
Your mother
Whatever she sought
Could she have found it
Here?
Then?
In such desolate wilderness?
As hard as African grass is
Tender
As bitter as African root is
Sweet
Toronto
All lean-tos and log cabins
Hysteria, mud and greed
The city hall a tent
A frontier town of beaten raging men
Fleeing Histories
Stalking a Future
Killing Indians already backed back into
Doom
The buffalo gone, the black pines bled white
But she was black and free.
She hauled timber
Burned dung chips and sod
Ate corn pone Indian style
Fought bears, snow and filth
Free
She fought thieves and vagabonds
Rapists, murderers
Slave kidnappers and bounty-hunters
Free.
Did she dream of Timbuktu?
Great-grandmother
Did you know?

5.

I remember
You
Anna
Your mother
I see her a ruby
Burnished red with Arab blood
Swiped with Portuguese
And God knows
What else
Rapists (All) the
All-Colonial-Melting-Pot
But from what place
Come echoes of Krishna?
From Zanzibar or beyond
The Indian Ocean?
Ghosts of Berbers
Hindu merchants and
Chinese sailors
Like waves washing a skin
That changed color
On different days
Delighting her husband
(Not your father)
Your father
You never knew
Orphan and madwoman
A black Botticelli
Rising whole out of an
African seashell
A stranger to that
Ex-slave cabin
And those stark Canadian nights
Great-grandmother
Did you know?

6.

I remember
You
Anna
You
Who mixed your strange and
Raging blood
Raga scented with
Islands and oceans with
Some Scottish farmer
Seeking warmth and sunlight
In your amber skin
Seeking respite from the wilderness in
Africa and India
Did you love this man?
Walking barefoot to that barren homestead
Your wedding dress strapped to your back
Clinging to a frightened heart
As you clung that night some twenty years ago
Did you love this man?
Pale and silent and Northern
Exhausted by Canadian winters
Who gave you your only child
Agnes
Fair and freckled farm girl
With dark eyes and red hair
White
Beautiful
At last
Isn't that what you wanted me to be?
Did you love this man?
Out of the Canadian winter?
Who gave you your only child
I try to find a face for him
A laugh, a voice, a walk
Great-grandmother
Did you know?

7.

I remember
You
Anna
Agnes
Who grew up in wheat fields
Alone
And fell back into
Blackness
In love
How you must have hated your son-in-law,
West
The biggest blackest handsomest
Man she'd ever seen
Poor farm girl Agnes
West
A foreigner
An American
Smelling of strange, mysterious places
A fine jive talking saxophone playing
Tambourine thumping
Bad-assed-jazz-musician from Philadelphia!
I've got to laugh
But she was happy
Happy.
Falling back with a vengeance
Back into Blackness
Back into the passionate embrace of the ghetto
Back from that lonely country farm to
San Francisco
Washington
Memphis
Chicago
New York
What strange and exotic places to her!
She never had to dream of Timbuktu!
Great-grandmother
Did you know?

8.

I remember
You
Anna
Agnes
Ran away with an American
And broke her father's heart
Turned it to stone
Against you both
Bad blood
Raging blood raga scented
With islands and oceans
Uncontrollable
Unpredictable
Uncivilized
Love!
There must have been some
Love!
Kid Ory/Fate Marable/Albert Nicholas
Papa Celestin
Love!
Zutty Singleton/Ollie Powers/Fletcher Henderson
Trixie Smith
Love!
King Oliver/Barney Bigard/Ma Rainey/Carroll Dickerson
Bessie Smith
Love!
Before Agnes came back the first of many times
To leave then reclaim and leave again
The fruit of her love
Oh Great-grandmother
Could you not have bent a bit for her?
And finally the last return, the ultimate exhaustion.
The two stones of your heart
Side by side in their wheat fields
Great-grandmother
Did you know?

9.

I remember
You
Anna
Agnes
Did she really intend
Her child to be raised by
The Sisters of the
Immaculate
Conception?
Vivian
Juice of such a wild and heathen
Ride
There was nothing
Immaculate
About her conception:
Some funky hotel for
Colored
Last exit of one-night stands
Blue walls neonkindled
Drums hardly stilled and
Tambourines!
How you must have hated
Your son-in-law
West
He dragged your Agnes
Back to Africa
And made her happy.
Happy.
Did she dream of her Canadian wheat fields
Riding the lonely night trains?
Did she whisper
Father!
In the deserted dawn
Still reeking tambourines?
Great-grandmother
Did you know?

10.

I remember
You
Anna
Agnes
Vivian
How they must have prayed over her
Those Sisters of the
Immaculate
Conception
Who had never known
Tambourines!
Who in the panting
Hysteria of their cells
Had never reached
That State of Grace called
Tambourines!
How they must have prayed
Over her
Leeching that insurrectionous blood
Raging and raga scented
You
Put there
Yourself
Anna
You
Who could not
Not have known love
It is in your strange and raging blood
Raga scented with
Oceans and islands
You must have lived love there
In the Canadian wilderness
With your farmer
You walked barefoot to
Great-grandmother
Did you know?

11.

I remember
You
Anna
Agnes
Vivian
Who limped out of her
Catholic cage
At seventeen
Looking for Life
Looking for her father
Loving him through all those
Hail Marys
Full of Grace
Dreaming of him through all those
Hail Marys
Full of Grace
Who limped out of her
Catholic cage
An atheist
Full of Grace
Full of Youth
Looking for her father
Finding him in Baltimore
Smelling of cigarettes and pride
Dying of chronic nephritis
Bestowing love too late
Vivian
Who limped out of her
Catholic cage
At seventeen
Undaunted by all those
Hail Marys
Full of Grace and
Ripe for Love
Great-grandmother
Did you know?

12.

I remember
You
Anna
Agnes
Vivian
I am the end
Of our line
A single row of wombs
Each with a single fruit
Was there another fate?
Some other destiny murdered
On that damnéd island
Zanzibar?
And thrown across
The Atlantic?
Did you live love in the
Canadian wilderness
Or did you dream it all?
Betrothed in your mother's womb
To some African kin
Marriage contract written
With a finger in fresh sand
Did you call out
That night long past
Clinging to a frightened heart
While stars rushed by:
Cousin!
I am
Gone!
Who was your mother?
Empress
And who was your father?
Orphan
And who am I?
Great-grandmother
Did you know?

13.

I remember
You
Anna
I walk this narrow brick alley
Named after you and
Look for myself
I come with someone you'd like
A friend
A lover
I try to see through this
White clapboard house
Into my beginnings
Any history will do
For those who have none
It seems you lived so long here
They named the street after you
McWard Street
House number seven
Kingston, Toronto
Ontario
Canada
The end of the line
Great-grandmother
Did you know?

LETTERS

I AWOKE IN THE SHAVED AND SULLEN HEAT

I awoke in the shaved and sullen heat
A castaway
Seeking land
Climbing to the foot of the bed
Curled around myself
Framed by night's
Black lacquered door
I watched you sleep
Flung out against white
By some wild pitch
Prancing in the half-turned profile
Of a male dancer on a
Priceless Greek vase
You slept on . . .
Through centuries
While I sat watch
And Luna came
And turned you over
And turned you again and again
As you dissolved
In a rash of fade-outs
On Aegean-blue film
Trapped forever
In the changing positions
Of a delicate ceramic frieze
I touched your curved and helpless hand
Tendered
And my heart froze
A dazzled tourist
In the sixth century
Before Christ.

I CLAIM THE BEAUTY OF YOU

I claim the beauty of you
For my own
David!
David!
Marble-veined and smoothed
How bright you are!
Can it be only
The disk of dawn light
Depending on how you turn
You seem . . .
Engraved
Gelatin sprinkled in delicate tones
Of etched gray
Submerged and
Emerging from
An acid bath
That can't dissolve stone
Nor love
Nor the space around you
Which seems
More dense
Than steel
You are so impossibly
Isolated
Yet even as you are modern
You remain
Marble
That ancient grip on immortality
That Michelangelo
Turned into a natural man
With a kiss.

I HAD WAITED . . .

I
Had
Waited
So
Long
For this
Finished
Some impossible march
Over mountains
I was tired.
My lungs ached
I
Turned my back
Against the sun
To read
Gingerly so as not to
Break in two or rather
Shatter into kaleidoscope
Patterns
Reflecting each word
As a tiny mirror reflects
A few poor colored fragments
Catapulting them into infinity
And the stained-glass
Complexity of
My Lady of Clery
How
Banal
A letter
Of
Love.

A POSTMARK FROM WHERE YOU ARE

A postmark
From where you are
Dread rises
Beaten back
By a desperate heart
Working like a nigger
To stop
Angst
That underbelly of
Love
Opening like Naias
In stagnant water
Round my legs that
Flee
The underbrush of
Doom
Torn and cut and bruised
Until I cannot
Stand but
Sit
And cannot sit but
Lay
My bones
Ground into
Tears that leave
Black
On my white linen
Black
On white stock
Words
Written in a fine, clear
And steady hand
Hands I've kissed
How many times?

YOU CAN'T DO THIS
TO ME
Silence
Red as
A postmark
From where you are

A WHITE SPACE

A white space
To be filled
Fat
Expensive
White paper
With a faint elegant
Watermark
Washed into
White again
As storms
Wash blue skies
White.
A white space
To be filled
The envelope
(Blue-lined of course)
Waiting to one side
Discreetly
A doorman averting his eyes
Too much love
Indecent
Supercilious
On the sidewalks of New York.
A white space

To be filled
Should I
Shed
One
Tear
And fold it
Neatly
Into four?

SPECIAL DELIVERY LETTER

Dropped
My
Left eye and
My
Right hand
Dropped them
Into
A hole black as jet
As hot and humid as
The mouth of a lion
A roaring in my ears
Salt
Sea-washed in
My
Mouth
Too late
Now
It's done
Anyway
Left
My left
Eye and
My

Right hand
Back
There
Running like the wind
Sand and grit in
My
Left eye and
My
Right hand
Don't look back
Tomorrow morning
He
Will touch
My
Left eye and hold
My
Right hand.

I KEPT THEM ALL

B.R. for M.R., December 25, 1971

I

I
Kept them
All.
Your letters.
Spilling out of old hat boxes
And cardboard boxes
And shoe boxes.
I feel like
Some cranky old archivist
At the Bibliothèque Nationale
Prisoner of

All this
Paper weight.
I should have burned them
All
Long ago
Like the Hindu burn their dead
So that their spirits rejoin
Time.
Letters.
Weight.
Our history.
Scribbled on anything, anywhere:
Airline stationery
Postcards, yellow legal-pad sheets
Rice paper, notebook paper, tissue paper;
Grainy beige hotel-drawer paper
Letterheads from every
Hotel, hostel, embassy
Inn, barroom, rest house
Garrison, airport, press club
Possible
A Michelin Guide to
War
Revolution
Famine
Danger
Death
Distance
I should have burned them
All
Long ago
So that their spirits rejoin
Time.

II

I remember the first
Leopoldville.

Lumumba lived.
It came and I didn't recognize
The hand.
Could it be that
Once
I didn't recognize that
Wide and sprawling down/beat
Hand
Full of violent, elegant
Strokes
Filling page after page with
No margins
Or rather
All margins
Filled with
More.
Leopoldville.
Lumumba lived
Your hand
That scattered my life like
Scrabble tiles
Rewording it in your own language
Intricate
Demanding
Fascinating and
Without parallel.
Leopoldville.
Lumumba lived.
I know.
You have him like some
Wild animal trophy
In your files.
What else came with you and those letters from
Leopoldville?
The scent of Africa:
The continent that belongs to me?
Perhaps I should have

Burned that first letter
Let my ancestors whisper to me from its ashes.
Blow the dark breath of Africa in my ear
Tell me stories I've never heard
Leopoldville.
Lumumba lived.

III

Letters answered/Letters
Letters followed/Letters
Please forward
Hold for arrival
If undelivered
Please
Return
To
Sender
You trailed paper like a bride
And I collected it like a streetcleaner
Gathering all the scraps
Into neat little stacks
Sorting postmarks like Morse Code:
Cable me
It is so hot here
Shower four times a day
Traveled by jeep
Bush country
Traveled by plane
Mountain rebels
Traveled by helicopter
Tired
Traveled by junk
Sick
Traveled on foot
Lost
The ambassador in Delhi
The AFP correspondent in Saigon

And guess what . . .
The weather
The Prime Minister
Miss you
Good dinner
Fantastically beautiful
Some crossfire
If only
Ruined film
Burned-out village
You were
Here
Torture
Airfreight
Come.

IV

I came.
Timidly at first
Like a child entering a room full of adults
Becoming bolder and bolder as
More and more
Sweets were offered
I flew on fed
Names I had only dreamed now
Falling easily from my lips
Arrogantly
With body posture
Like jive talk
In Harlem
Kashmir and Khartoum
Algiers, Odessa, Aswan, Andorra,
Alexandria, New Delhi

Darling

Delphi, Istanbul, Parma, Phnom Penh
Addis Ababa, Katmandou
Luxor, Moscow, Nairobi, Conakry, Hsilinhaote

Hold

Hanoi
Talcapolco
Angkor Vat, Caledonia, Calcutta
Marseilles, Suez, Shanghai
Positano, Valparaiso
Spoleto, Siena, Sian
Dakar, Abidjan, Milan

My

Marrakech, Mozambique, Chenonceaux
Dar Es Salaam, Leningrad, Houston

Hand

Houhehote, Venice, Karnak
Peking
I stuffed myself
A child bride on her
Wedding day
Fingers henna-dipped
Eyes black-rimmed and avid
Bejeweled and still
Invisible
To her
Husband

v

Husband
Will there be
A
Last
Letter
You
&
I?
You will let me know?
(Of course)
You will let me know?
(Of course)

Pick a beautiful place
(There are so many)
To
Let
Me
Go.
I've gone
So far with you
Trailed years after me
Like baggage tags strewn on lonely winds
Pick some oasis in the Sahara
Azaona, for example
Or the foot of the pyramid at Thebes
(Did I really meet you there?)
How
Im-
Possible
Or choose Wadi Halfa or
Kilimanjaro
Why not?
We've been to better places together
And left them behind
Without so much
As a backward glance
All I know is
I want to die on my continent
I want to die in Brazzaville.
Or pick a place that has
No History at all.
Pick
Oum Chalouba
I'll expect you.

THE ANSWER

Darling
Sian is in
Heat
The vet was
Very cross
He said I shouldn't be
Surprised by
Her
Heats
And
I should have had
Shots given to her
Every six months
He said
It was too late to do
Anything
And
I was to give her
Sugar lumps with
Tranquilizers in them
And put
Eau de Cologne
On her
Bottom.
Tranquilized
Sugar lumps
And
Eau de Cologne
Man's
Answer
To
Woman's
Heats.

TO GLORIA

Dear
Gloria
Steinem
I have
A
Problem
I
Am
Female
And
I
Am
Lib-
Erated
But
I would rather be
Beau-
Tiful
Than
Not
I
Would rather be
Made love to
Than
Not
I
Would rather be
Lover
Than
Friend
In
Other
Words
I
Am

A
Backsliding
Man-loving
Crotch-gazing
Phallus-adoring
Counter-revolutionary
Renegade
Handkerchief head
Sexist
Slave
I feel like some
Good nigger
Southern white folks
Haul out to
Prove
Their niggers
Are
Happy
Niggers
Some liver-lipped
Honky loving
Uncle Tom
Rolling my eyes
(contact lenses by Horning and Colt)
And
Shuffling my feet
(loafers by Gucci)
Shaking my lips like tambourines
(dress by Pucci)
Knocking my knees in a Gospel jump
(body stocking by Christian Dior)
My carpetbag rattling
(Louis Vuitton)
My hands clapping
(nails: Revlon; rings: Tiffany's;
watch: Piaget; gloves: Hermes)
Rolling on the ground

(fur rug by Jacques Kaplan)
And shouting to high Heaven
(gargle by Listerine)
Teeth grinding
(caps by Dr. Klaie)
Hopping and sweating
(deodorant by Vichy)
Throwing myself around
(perfume by Guerlain)
In the burning bush of a
Southern sun
(sun-glasses by Givenchy)
Head ticking
(hair spray by Coty)
A Sunday bone-crack
(shampoo by Carita)
Bandana
(by Pierre Cardin)
Waving like a witch doctor's
Monkey fur switch
(got to get me one)
Gloria
I
Just
Can't
Seem
To
Get
The
Hang
Of it
Trembling at some
Baritone voice
Gut-snapping at some
Broad-shouldered
Embrace
Swooning at some

Sycophant's mustached
Kiss
I
Am
The
Absurdity of
Absurdities
A
Backsliding
Man-loving
Crotch-gazing
Phallus-adoring
Counter-revolutionary
Renegade
A handkerchief head
Sexist
Slave
Gloria!
Hold
My
Hand.

HOW DO I SAY

How do I say
I love you
Without sounding trite
Or childish or hysterical
Or sick
I've tried telegrams and phone calls
Postcards and your answering service
But always
That wary and jaded eye

That patronizing misanthropic mouth
Stops me.
I think:
How would that look in print?
Can it be that
The New York Review of Books
Can come
Between
People?

LA CHENILLÈRE I

You
Celebrate well
In all seasons
Like one good wine

Summer light
Low and tender
Powdered and delicate
Linden-tree leaves trembling
I saw
Three wild swans
The other day
Two white and
One black

Summer light
Low and tender
Floating in silence
Only low flying
Swallows and
Now and again a

Wild duck or
A swamp gull
Water skiing

Summer light
Low and tender
Quiet black
Non-reflecting water
Fretted with
Silver coins
We've been having
Rainstorms with
Bursts of sunshine

Summer light
Low and tender
Suddenly
The sky darkens like a rash
Then as suddenly
A burst of yellow
A spotlight
Casting long and navy shadows
On white stone walls

You
Celebrate well
In all seasons
Like one good wine

LA CHENILLÈRE II

You
Celebrate well

In all seasons
Like one good wine

But you are best
Now
In November
Cracked like Chinese porcelain
Brittle as blown crystal
Swept with curling leaves
Scattered like hysterical kisses
That have lost their power to convince
Covered with naked vines
That have lost the regency of love
Revealing a permanent paradisiacal embrace
Of cloying tentacles.

You are best
Now
In November
When bullets riffle and rattle the dawn
And quail and partridge scream
Hunted by beasts of both sorts
Treading the flesh and bone of pine cones underfoot
When rid of that vulgar summer green blanket
That molds and softens like a woman's make-up
Nude, you rest under the rapt and skeletal gaze of winter
Under the same futile and furious scrutiny
That one day one turns on one's own life

At the point
Where
It begins
To end.

PEKING

ON THE TERRACE AT 11 NAN CHIHTZE STREET

Standing
On somebody's terrace
Feeling foreign
Gazing at a city more like a Universe Forbidden
Rising over Peking like flamingo wings a
Hovering which is neither float nor flight
But a murmuring static in the still air
The roofs of palaces and pavilions catching the last
Light as if the sun were their own reflection
Corner towers rise to meet the descending mist
Which becomes a pale and smoky screen
Between the red walls of the city and my avid Western eyes
Like the veils the emperor's valets wore
So as not to contaminate him with their breath
A breeze sweeps the moat as if a Chinese character brush
Correctly poised, dipped expertly into ink
The Eastern Gate shuts with a hollow ring and a cry
Hawk sparrows maneuver in the dusk
Pale lights snap on girding the yellow mall in a beaded belt
Flattening passing navy figures into relief-less shadows
Half hidden by willows breeze-bent in oriental kowtow to the
Western Wind blowing off the Gobi desert bringing sand
And lifting clouds of ever-present Peking dust that scuttles by
Chinese conversation, soft and dissonant lying below and about
Scraped dishes echo off tiled walls like keys rattling
And here and there a stubborn child lingers outside
Savoring the last swooning daylight before bed while I,
Standing
On somebody's terrace
Feeling foreign
Gazing at a city more like a Universe Forbidden
Resist until the light leaps away.

THE DIVORCE OF COMRADE WU AND COMRADE LUI

I

The divorce of Comrade Wu and Comrade Lui
Was very banal indeed
And oddly enough
Came about on a Sunday
Through no fault
Of their own
Merely
Because neither of them was willing
To waste a day off
On a
Divorce.
The Revolutionary Committee of Factory Number 4
(The Shining Sun Paint factory)
Decided once
And for all
The issue
Comrade Wu and Comrade Lui
Would both take off a day from work
Sunday, the 10th of May
The year of our Lord 1965
The year sixteen of the Revolution
And so this day
They eat fried noodles
In silence
In celebration?
The prisoner's last meal
And Comrade Wu stares at her yellow walls
With the poster of Mao Tse-tung
Hung there
And wonders
"Who will get the flat?
Who will get the flat?"
And Comrade Lui stares at Comrade Wu and thinks:

"How long before I marry my love?
How long before I marry my love?"
And outside the Peking winter breaks
Against the window pane
Humidifying it hopelessly
Running down it haphazardly
And inside the cotton curtains stick cloyingly to it
Like a shirt sticking to a man's back on a hot day
And outside the silhouettes of Comrade Wu and Comrade Lui
Glisten in frosted silence
And inside the central heating hisses
A Chinese vowel
As morning sounds infiltrate the paper-thin partitions.
Coughs and sneezes and morning-exercise music
Mingle in the dehydrated air
As slowly Comrade Wu gets up to do her morning
Tai chi chuan
As slowly Comrade Wu gets up to
Say her imperturbable
And tight-lipped farewell
In transfixed slow motion
As together
They carry the tiger on the mountain
And together
They part the wild horse's mane on the right
A flickering film of a pinpoint
On the bottom of the sea
Gliding and floating in the yellow room
Like goldfish
Tails flapping in desperate directional starts at
Breaking out of pain's circle
Thus, they finish
The last morning together
And together they leave
Locking the door and walking slowly
To their bicycles leaning unchained
In the front hall

Comrade Lui letting Comrade Wu pass in front
As silently they move onto the dusty road
And into the wide avenue
Rowdy with morning bicycle traffic
Dodging insolent pedestrians
They pedal silently side by side
The last ride.

II

Wordlessly they arrive
In the chilly unthawed morning
At 17 Nan Chu Street,
The Department of Family and Welfare
And are greeted by a neutral-eyed clerk
Who informs them
They are
Nine minutes late
Before they can
Excuse themselves
Already beginning to sweat
In their heavy winter coats
(Comrade Lui's glasses
Steaming up)
A shadow behind a frosted glass door
Opens it and beckons them forward
Comrade Lui passes
In front of
Comrade Wu
In his nervousness
And sits on one of the stiff-backed chairs
As if settling in
For a bad meal
And Comrade Wu, entering
Seems to startle him
As if she wasn't expected
And he rises only half way
Compressing his knees

To let her by
As she brushes him with
The backs
Of hers
As if there wasn't
Twenty meters
Of gray limestone space
In front of her
And seated beside him
Separated by the width of a double bed
She notices the courtroom
Is painted the same yellow
As her kitchen
(That 1963 surplus of yellow paint
At the Shining Sun Paint Factory)
And thinks:
"Who will get the flat?
Who will get the flat?"
And Comrade Lui
Stares straight ahead and thinks:
"When will I marry my love?
When will I marry my love?"
And the yellow walls
And the limestone floor
Glow in white neon iridescence while
The central heating hisses a
Chinese vowel
And the tribunal files in
Behind a high and heavy podium
Fashioned in 1940
Bureaucratic modern
With a red star
In the center
Two men
One woman
And a woman scribe
Their names neatly printed on

White cards
Before their seats
The last
Dinner party.
And the chairman
His tinted glasses flashing
In a brief laser beam
Of pale sunlight
Clears his throat
Under a portrait of
Mao Tse-tung
Hung there
And begins.

III

And like two swimmers
In the Yangtze
Comrade Wu and Comrade Lui struggle through
Depths and currents of compromise
Tides and undertows of dailiness
Waves and breakers of desire
Rocks and reefs of ego
Gales and stiff winds of pride
Like two soldiers on the Long March
They labor over
Mounds of resentment and disappointment
Canyons of boredom and misunderstandings
Summits of mistakes and miscellaneous
Precipices of money and in-laws
Crevices of dependence and lies
Gorges of defeat and recriminations
Sitting in their straight-back chairs
Sweating in their winter coats
Separated by the width of a double bed
They swim
And they climb
Breathing deliberately

Comrade Wu twists her handkerchief in small pale hands
Comrade Lui's strong brown ones
Rest spread out on his knees
Deputy One insists
On a definition of
Corporal punishment
His pale scalp gleaming out of short cropped hair
Deputy Two
Shuffles papers from
One delicate hand to the other
And asks:
"When did sexual relations stop?"
And Comrade Wu catches the eye of
Chairman Chou
(So his place card says)
And asks with her eyes in no uncertain terms
"Who will get the flat?
Who will get the flat?"
But the chairman, who lights up a cigarette
And whose eyes are obscured by
Rose-tinted glasses
Merely asks how much money she makes
And Comrade Lui slumps beneath his second
Matrimonial disaster
The visor of his cap
Tilting like a sinking ship
And it is over.
Two men
One woman
And a woman scribe
Rise and announce
The case closed
Doors open and shut
Shadows fuzz and frost
Feet shuffle on limestone
Throats clear
While the central heating hisses a

Chinese vowel
And Comrade Wu makes a humming sound
Between her teeth
And Comrade Lui watches the black-shod feet
Of his wife
Propel themselves like tiny boats
Beside his own
Forever
And beyond his own
Forever
Onto the dusty concrete of
Forever
And Comrade Lui
Looks up into the creaking sunlight
Groaning down the Peking street
Whose long gray walls
Stretch on and on
Forever
On both sides.

I SAW A CHINESE LADY . . .

I saw a small Chinese lady with bound feet in the park
Hobbling down a pale drenched trail of mimosa early in the day
Eyes blank with dotage and reminiscence
Feet like an unfinished drawing running off the page:
The dots of black baggy trouser exclamation points

Domino fetish feet, white-socked and black-shod *Golden Lilies*
Anachronism of anachronisms, recalling History like an out-
dated penny
No longer acceptable as the coin of the realm
But cherished as a souvenir of a past not to be denied
And given to children to play with.

SMILING MAO

Smiling Mao, Mao smiling
Mao smiling Mao and Mao
smiling smiling Mao smiling

Thoughts having become
The center of the world
Thoughts having become
The only thoughts worth
Thinking as thoughts
Thoughts, thought
As thoughts have
Never been thought before
Held as thoughts have
Never been held before:
As a guard and a bandage as
A production report and
A prayer, as a love song
And a children's chant
Thoughts added up
In billions
Eight hundred million
Thoughts based on
The same thoughts make
A multitude of thoughts
A cosmic force
To be reckoned with
With some
Thoughts of our own.

Smiling Mao, Mao smiling
Mao smiling Mao and Mao
smiling smiling Mao smiling

HANGCHOW

Your bodies barely touch
White pigeon pairs
Dark sleek heads bent
Converging into starched shirts
Grating against one another
While Spring hovers round you
Like silk drapery kissing necks
With sweet stirrings of summer

Your bodies barely touch
White pigeon pairs
Test-tube babies of the
Cultural Revolution
Sitting beside this poet's lake
Perched quietly beneath age-trellised trees
That drop pollen on
White cotton shoulders

Your bodies barely touch
White pigeon pairs
As you whisper with chaste lips
What?
Comrade?
While the Western Lake dreams on like a curse
And love
That fanatic's joke lurches by.

SNEAKING AROUND CORNERS

Sneaking around corners
As noncommittal as a Chinese smile,

A Peking wall slides by bland in neutral gray
Punctuated by a jade-green door like
A parenthesis in a long paragraph.

SHANGHAI

Tender-faced soldiers walking hand in hand
And Girls Afraid to Look in Their Mirrors.

SOFT-SHELL CRABS STEAMING

Soft-shell crabs
Steaming in woven baskets over hot coals
Smells threading in and out of consciousness bringing
Saliva to the mouths of blue quilted workers
Swaying in the breeze like April irises
Scraps of conversation rise on
Sinuating heat like kites over
Stalls on Lui Li Chen Street and the
Scented song of the vendor
Sighs on in the
Soft evening of a Peking
Spring.

FLYING A KITE

For Alexis

Flying
a
kite
in
the
People's
Park
of
Peking is
like
flying
a
kite
no where
else
in
this
w
o
r
l
d

People
of f
hundreds l
ying
are
kites
there
in
Because
the
People's
Park
of
Peking.

TAI LAKE STONE

Dignified Surrealism
Raised to Art on Ming Wings
Gliding in and out of centuries
Like the Empress Wu's stone ship
Staring like some Mongolian watchdog
Sent to sic the barbarians.

IF ONE SETS ONE'S FOOT

If one sets one's foot
  At zero and starts walking
    Forward into Time and
      Around Time and beneath
        Time and on top of Time
          Traveling a great wide
        Road of centuries, a
      Coiling callus across
    The world haunted by
  Thousand-year-old ghosts
    Stationed like toll-
      Booths on that scaly
        Expressway, eight-laned
          And beholden to no one
        Speckled with well-behaved
      People promenading every
    Sunday on Xenophobia's
  Most extravagant shrine.

MAO WAVED TO THE PEOPLE

Mao waved to the People
That curious ripple from
Little finger to
Index finger
And back again
And
The People
Waved
Back.

PONIES . . .

Ponies
Ponies
Scattered
Scattered
On the
On the
Steppes
Steppes
Serenity
Your name is
Your name is
Space
Space
Ponies
Scattered
On the
Steppes
Serenity
Your name is
Space

LETTER FROM MONGOLIA

Saffron light
Filtered down through the navel of this
Brown felt womb
Squatting in this Mongolian yurt
In this Mongolian place
Whose very name is
The end of the world
The taste of cosmos on my lips
Rancid butter and milk and strong tea as
Unknown tongues ricochet off soft
Multicolored carpets
Blending into God knows
What hypermetrical of sounds
And God knows how my sparse and angular
English weaves in and out
Of this tunnel
Emerging from the other side
Only to make the return journey
Like some desperate commuter
Stuck forever in the Lincoln Tunnel
For our Han interpreter speaks no Mongolian
And our Mongolian guide speaks no Han
And I speak neither
So we continue
Linked like worry beads
To communicate with nods and smiles
With body language as if
Touch could tell
Squeezed between Han and Mongol
Our blue quilted pajamas like
Stuffed cotton buffers:
A no-man's-land of language
Between the frontiers of hostile countries

I gaze at a portrait of Mao
Absently, like a swaying passenger

Reading advertisements in the subway
A transistor radio
An alarm clock made in Hong Kong
A packet of Chinese cigarettes
A newspaper, a box of Shanghai matches
A plastic vase with artificial flowers.
A portrait of Mao
A Mongol matron
Sitting to the left of me
Cuts mutton for her guests
These strange and clumsy Hans
With their barbarians from the West
What can you think of me
Mongol matron
With your small and delicate wrists gold-ringed
The sleeves of your quilted robe
Flung back absently
Mongol matron
Whose men speak in epic poetry
Like the American Indians
Your race's name alone
Is still enough to strike terror in white hearts
What a saving grace
To strike terror in the bloated and cholesteroled heart
Of Western Europe
Mongol matron
Serene in the absoluteness of change
I can tell by the set of that mouth
The grace of those tattooed hands
The line of that restless back
You will never sleep in a stone house

You'll never rest your head
Beneath brick and concrete
Nor let your men
Who speak in epic poetry
Like the American Indians
Do so while you have breath

To breathe this purest light
That some call isolation:
I try telepathy to reach through
Your blue quilts and mine
Stare into your fine-boned face
Purified by space
Transfixed by solitude
Primed on desolation
Glowing in the evening of the
End of the world like a penny.
Almond eyes as deep and blank
As a night out there under the stars
A mouth used to saying nothing
A skin as wind-polished as
Siberian rock
As golden as winter grass
Darkening against the white turban
Flattening long black hair
Mongol matron
Raising your eyes from time to time
To greet your husband opposite you
Raising your eyes with just the vaguest
Appeal for approval from a round-faced shepherd
In brown quilt to the ground and
Fine soft crimson leather boots
Who smiles reassuringly
While outside sheep are sprinkled like salt on the brown steppes.

THE WELL OF THE PRECIOUS CONCUBINE PEARL

Can it be that the world is not flat?
As level as stagnant water in brass urns
Spaced on marble terraces as steady as sin?

Roof tiles threaded like golden sea shells
Curved like a queen's haunch
Marble terraces mounting like fate
As horizon-less as the sea
So deadly smooth as to seem
Anchored to the center of the world
Loneliness riveted like ice caps
Onto the eye of the world
And the eye of the world is in
The Well of the Precious Concubine Pearl

Dragons and Phoenix rising on
Marble terraces mounting like desire
Hauled by ten thousand elephants
Carved by ten thousand eunuchs
The nameless whose bones are mortar for the
Four brick walls enclosing four brick walls
Each square a ripple in a well
In the eye of the world
And the eye of the world is in
The Well of the Precious Concubine Pearl

Courtyards radiate outwards on a silken thread
To be pulled back like delicate regulatory weights
Tender balance of texture
Whole justice of line
Singular exhortation of perspective
Shooting breath across transparent vastness
The opening and closing of gates like lungs
The opening and closing of gates like lungs
The opening and closing of love like gates
The opening and closing of love like gates

Shadows of a million coolies
Stir the depths of the Golden River Canal
Spanned by three marble bridges
As truly arched as the perfect brow of a child

Pure of all contrivances yet cunning in absoluteness
The true innocence of space
The opening and closing of gates like lungs
The opening and closing of gates like lungs
The opening and closing of love like gates
The opening and closing of love like gates

The Gate of Culmination
The Gate of Supreme Harmony
The Gate of Eastern Blowing
The opening and closing of love like gates
The opening and closing of love like gates
The Gate of Integrity in Order
The Gate of Transcendent Accord
The Gate of Serenity in Old Age
Love rustles in gray silk in the palace
Love rustles in gray silk in the palace

Love rustles in gray silk in the palace
Love rustles in gray silk in the palace
The Palace of Dazzling Clarity
The Palace of Purity in Affection
The Palace of Delicious Things
The Palace of Infinite Pleasure
The Palace of Potent Fecundity
The Palace Where One Gives Thanks for a Son
The Palace of Perfect Peace
The Palace of Literary Glory

Love rustles in gray silk in the palace
Love rustles in gray silk in the palace
The Palace of Buddha
The Palace of Tranquility And Quietude
The Palace of Eternal Spring
The Palace of Intellectual Refinement
The Palace of Total Joy
The Palace of Rare Sublimeness

The Palace of Ultimate Elegance
The Palace of The Certitude of Happiness

And in the pavilion
Black hair shifts
Black hair shifts in the pavilion
And white porcelain cracks
In the Pavilion of the Purest Perfumes
In the Pavilion of Melodious Sounds
Black hair shifts
And white porcelain cracks
On a red lacquered table
Spilling tea leaves

Onto the eye of the world
And the eye of the world is in
The Well of the Precious Concubine Pearl.

HAN SHROUD

Jade
God's juices
Solidified
Shield against mortality
I cover you drop by drop
Like grains of rice
Run from
The silos of my favorite
domain
I cover you as
I covered you in life
With my body still warm
From the hunt
Ardent heat
Now

Jade
Love's juices
Solidified
Smooth as your own flesh
I cover you drop by drop
Like emerald perfume
Running from
My favorite silver and ivory
gourd
I cover you as
I covered you in life
With my body still warm
From the sun of my terrace
Ardent heat
Now

As cold as
These jade fragments
I weave
With golden threads
Round you
Beloved wife
Princess!

Jade
Power over life and death
Solidified
Imperial seals of the Middle
  Kingdom
I'd forgotten
Emperors die too
We are side by side but
I am too weighted down with
  winding sheet
To take your hand
Too weighted with jade
To move my heart
Jade closes my eyes and my
  nostrils
This suffocating green
That prevents me from seeing
My empress
Love
Take this mask from me
So that I may see your face
For the last time
Beloved friend
Princess!

As cold as
These jade fragments
I weave
With golden threads
Round you
Beloved husband
Prince!

Jade
The green of June wheat
Solidified
As tender as my silks brushing
  your hand
I'd forgotten
Empresses die too
We are side by side but
I am too weighted down with
  winding sheet
To take your hand
Too weighted with jade
To move my heart
Jade closes my eyes and my
  nostrils
This lily-leaf green
That prevents me from seeing
My emperor
Love
Take this mask from me
So that I may see your face
For the last time
Beloved friend
Prince!

[Dedicated to Mary McCarthy
with thanks for her support and encouragement
at a decisive moment for this book.
B.C.R., Paris, November 1, 1973]

WHITE PORCELAINS

AND OUT OF LOVE

And out of love
Seated
She birthed
What Arp considered
Perfection
Between black thighs
It dropped
Baked by womb fires
Glazed with ambrosia
Swollen on Goddess juice
Egg-shaped
In white porcelain
It left her
Floating on the surface of
Primordial nebula
Neither sky nor sea
Neither space nor void
Neither matter nor
Anti-matter
But a cosmic cloud
Illuminated by Hell's
Original light
Rinsed with dry ice and
Flowing like a river of agate
Carried on the backs of
Albino elephants
Pawing primeval rain forests where
Peonies and pomegranates
Grow in groves
And the ivory serpent
Divides herself in two
And two again
In never-ending copulation
Which we, in pale imitation
Usurp

Shadow boxing on
Love's friezes
Like greedy heartless
Savage children
Scrawling precocious graffiti
On the garden walls
Of Earthly Delights.

HEADS BENT

Heads bent
As if over some
Mathematical problem
Hands sliding and trembling
On drug-glazed skin
Smoother than baked white porcelain
Cracked and fissured with
Uninvented lies
Burnt on flesh as on parchment
Scrupulously engraved
In delicate gold-embossed tones
By meticulous chaste and well-trained hands
Eyes gone blind from beauty
A labor of love
A work of years
The Book of Hours
Raging beyond form and color
Or rather
Inside form and made of color
Itself
As if the measure of Time
Hadn't been invented by the Egyptians
Did not float

Through immortal airless tombs
Love
Written on the ceiling made to believe
The cool taste of blue-green
Hovering between lips
Sighing on neon moonlight
A gleam of rose behind eyelids
Weighted by jade:
That green again
Interrupted by a wavy finger
Rumpling it and whipping up
Yellow smog that hides
Like a muslin mask
The one face I need to see
In this first light of a new day:
Your face
As we slip past each other into
Our respective
Solitudes.

IN DARKNESS I LIE

In darkness I lie
And hold your wrist
And take your pulse
A slow and passionate lapping
At my side
Steady as wave-breaking
On a stolen stone beach
The pulse of a soldier
Stalking land mines
The wary wait
For the flesh's flash

That exploding
White porcelain shell
Illuminating the night like
The back of Ahab's
White whale
Breaking the waters
Of this rare calm.
In danger, I lie
And kiss this sweet throbbing
And hold it to my lips
The vain underground
Of your body sweeps by
My breath
X-raying the convoluting
Freeways of secret arteries
Trafficking endlessly between
Existence and nonexistence
Veiled and taut skin hovering between
Man and Beast
Consciousness and nonconsciousness
While I explore
That vast inner space
As wild and inexplicable as
Those billion other stars
My lips placed like
One footprint on a moon
Trapped by a gravitational force
As irresistible as
What is described as
Love
Which makes me think:
I must change my life.

SING TO ME

Sing to me
Sing to me
Sing to me a sad song
And let my tears
As transparent as
White porcelain
As pure as
Uncontaminated moon
Venus-shaped and softly fluted
The lips curled back
By dragon's teeth
Bathe you
Bathe
Bathe, I say in
My million
White porcelain tears
Light-rounded and
Back-lit by fistfuls of diamonds
Falling one by one like
One million blows
If I were to count them
On ribs creaking under
A weight
So unwarranted
My heart
Has long since lost
Its senses
Speaking to the left
And to the right
No longer knowing what is real
And what is unreal
And no longer caring
Either
No longer knowing what is true
And what is untrue

And no longer caring
Either
Remembering only
What came before:
That great feast
Which was withdrawn
While I sang

BODY POISED

Body poised
Like an incandescent arrow
In the nacreous light
Pointing away
Leaving me
Leaving me
Shaking your head
In childish refusal to accept
Compromise
Condescending
Your last kisses that
Scorch my hair and singe my lashes
Already wet
I smell it (even now):
A hot iron on damp cloth
Kisses that bake my eyes into
White porcelain
As dead as Nefertiti's stare
At dusty walls
In Cairo
For moments I don't breathe
Thinking if I never move
You may stay

So I leave myself without breath
Without that reflex bellowing of the lungs
And you stay
But abstractly
As if you had
Other things on your mind
You lie down beside me
On a bright blade of morning
Quivering like a bow abruptly released
Leaving me
Leaving me
But why?
Will you rest easier
When you pass no more this way?
When you pass by Tel-el-Amarna?
Loneliness
Your name a thousand years
Still stands for
Everything.

LET ME LIE DOWN IN RED

Let me lie down in red
And let the beasts fly over me
Glowing in the wee hours
Like a blind eye
A white porcelain baptismal cradles
The red Chinese seal
I engrave there alone
Hung over and mesmerized by
A dazzling display of
Calligraphy
Slipping and sliding in

Prodigious configurations
Of beauty bloodied
Red on white
My wrists held before me
Like a handcuffed prisoner
A dangerous criminal
With murder in his heart
But not another's
Bracelets not of steel
But steel could not hold them
As fast and steady as this;
That I shake not
In this ridiculous mirrored palace
Of conspicuous consumption
Where I see myself
A hysterical fool
An aging child
A desperate delinquent
A cuckolded believer
Doing imagined violence
To myself
Into infinity
Transmigrated a thousand times
Over a thousand years
For a thousand different reasons
And I've not learned
Anything
And I've not forgotten
Anything
And I've not forgiven
Anything.

I GATHER

I gather
Cold white porcelain beads
Of mortal fatigue
As a child gathers spring violets
In bliss and yet in vague and
Unconscious destruction
Hands that are innocent yet guilty
Break the stems and tear out
The roots of creation
As if I had created myself
Could claim to be an invention
I am responsible for
And not, like some wonder drug
Made by mistake
While searching for
A cure for
Something else
My cure has long since been discovered
Was discovered with the world in fact
Was discovered in the fruit and bees of Babylon
Under the volcano of Chimborazo
Behind the columns at Karnak
Beneath the arches of Stonehenge
Buried in the tombs of Yucatan
Drowned in the waters of the Blue Nile
Frozen in Kilimanjaro
Fashioned in gold in Phoenicia
Chased in silver in Tibet
I have come to know it all
And to believe it
And will say it
If there are any to listen
Will even preach it although an atheist
And a bit embarrassed
Would my face burning recite the litanies

Say a year of rosaries
And a century of hail Krishnas
Would fall upon my prayer rug
Mend my tallith
Kiss the leper
If only death were not the root of life
Amnesia
Its bitter flower

DAWN IS CRACKLED

Dawn is crackled
Like an inverted
White porcelain bowl
Underglazed in
Ripe streaks of red which make
A marriage canopy
Over my head
Except
I am
No bride.
Chilled by the cold saliva
Of low-cut grass on bare feet
Very exclusive &
Sentimental meetings
Come back to me
Resurrected in this
Word-less not-night
Reincarnated in the posture
Of night animals
Now stilled
Very exclusive &
Sentimental meetings

Come back to me
Radar-guided
Through the cosmos
Of my nodding bones
Like a romp of stars
Positioning themselves
For today's horoscope: June 26
Affairs of the heart
For Cancers
Will be rather tepid
Today
Not so much
On your side
As on that of the
Other party
Concerned
So it might be
Just as well
To sidestep
Sentimental meetings.

WHITE PORCELAIN INK POT

White porcelain ink pot
Round gleaming and smooth
As O's history
The Magic Circle
Resting like a miniature moon frozen
On polished black teak
Split by a thin red line
Opening like a pomegranate revealing
Deadly red poison paste
(a nice touch that)

Passively waiting to receive the imprint
Of carved phallic seals
Proclaiming the identity
Of someone not supposed to die
Unaccompanied
Passively waiting to receive
Those compendious symbols
Of man's idea of himself
(civilization)
Carved in delicate ivory
Imperious marble
Majestic jade
Regal turquoise
Imperial emerald
Noble bronze
Stately quartz
Politicians scholars and senators
Poets princes and generals
Ministers bankers and judges
Priests philosophers and scientists
All transfixed into the pages of History
(History's idea of itself)
Reversed
(a nice touch that)
Power reversed and perversed by that
Poisonous thin red line
Each successive impress
Effaced by the one which follows
Banker erasing Prince erasing Poet
White porcelain ink pot
(History's whore).

CURVING LIKE A COLORLESS VASARELY

Curving like a colorless Vasarely
Glistening white tiles
Shimmy down an endless tunnel of
White hallucinations
Edged with shiny platinum pain
At the end of this tunnel not light
But my own blackness
Curling inwards like a slow
Cigarette burn in white paper
Crackling and contracting with
My contractions
Folding itself into flapping
White linen sails
Making that peculiar sound
Of wet canvas in high winds
Crashing in my ears as the lead anchor
Scrapes across mahogany planks and
Plunges into what depths
Sinking into white coral and
Holding
Holding
While effervescent shapes reach round me
Like archangels in the ozone landscape
Bringing me back
Brought back alive by
Gleaming figurines fashioned in
Pompadour's white porcelain
Oh!
The pomposity of it all
A Louis XIV court accouchement
I think of Rimbaud:
You are making a mistake
I am not of your race
I am of the race that

Sang under torture
I am of the race that
Births alone
On river banks of
Deep green moss
Staring wide-eyed
At the tilting
African sun.

ORGANDY CURTAINS SHIFTING

Organdy curtains shifting
In a rosy June breath
Muzzling a shepherdess, a Cheshire cat
My cherished figurines of white porcelain
Sitting in halcyon solitude
In the dappled unfocused light
Of my fifteenth summer
City heat rushing through
The narrow Victorian house
With the neat red-brick alley
As I lay dreaming on my organdy-covered virgin's bed
My grandmother
Entered my room without knocking
A freshly painted Renoir
A universe of firm voluptuous flesh
I'm dying
Was the only thing she said
And she wept.
And for the first time
In my childish mind's eye
I recalled her Christian name:
Elizabeth

A dying Elizabeth
Known to me until that moment as Mouf-mummy
I'm dying
Was the only thing she said
And she wept.
And Death like a slow blush stalked
The high-canopied bed where we sat
And I my unused womb
Free from Death's dealings
Held in my arms
The trembling flesh of my flesh
And rocked the rock of my life
Burned away in desperate and demented
Radiology
A virgin no more
My organdy-covered virgin's bed
Forever stained as I
Looked into the eyes
Of a dying woman I loved
And saw myself.

AN ALMOST FULL MOON

An almost full moon
Missing a tiny sliver
Coquettishly like a
Plucked eyebrow
Tongues still water
As I walk the shores of my own blight:
A hopeless territory of
Helpless dependence
The splinter off the moon
Resting on my naval like
The moon of your thumb as

I circle this forlorn lake
Reflecting the hostile indifferent
White porcelain landscape
Of another planet
The words, the music, as incomprehensible
As the tongues of aborigines
The mauve swish of bat wings and
The cries of wild geese
The whistles of sleepwalking nightingales
And masturbating crickets
Stir not Pity but Terror
A Greek chorus lamenting
My blithe miscalculation:
A perfectly respectable mathematical formula
That doesn't come out right at all
Filling a whole chilly planetarium
With desperate frantic equations, erased
Rewritten, repeated, reversed, tabulated
Added, multiplied, divided, subtracted, scribbled over
Revised, calculated, checked, canceled
Double-checked, squared and rooted to the nth degree
While a howling computer
Crouches laughing in the corner as
My hand trembles in defeat
My heart squeezed in the horror
Of some fundamental step ignored in the beginning
Some primary rule forgotten in the haste
To get on with it
Now searching back in panic
Trying to find the irremediable error
As the dry hot chalk of murder
Screeches across night's blackboard.

ABOUT THE AUTHOR

BARBARA CHASE-RIBOUD is an internationally known American sculptor—born and raised in Philadelphia. This collection is her debut in poetry, which, says Ms. Riboud, "is very close to a discipline both familiar and dear to me: drawing. Both are dangerous searches for perfection . . . drawing prepared me for the demands of poetry, but nothing prepared me for the joy of writing it."

Ms. Riboud lives in Paris with her husband and two sons.